NATIONAL
GE

Groups
of Animals

Greg Pyers

Contents

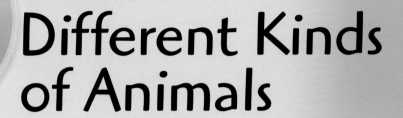

Different Kinds of Animals

There are millions of kinds of animals in the world. Some of these animals are **vertebrates**. A vertebrate is an animal with a backbone.

backbone

Animals can be sorted into groups, or classified. This book is about the five groups of vertebrates. They are reptiles, fish, amphibians, birds, and mammals.

Reptiles

Reptiles are one group of animals.
Lizards, snakes, crocodiles, and turtles are all reptiles. Reptiles are **cold-blooded**. This means that their body temperature changes with the temperature around them. In cool weather, some reptiles lie in the sun to warm up. Reptiles' bodies are covered with scales.

You can see the scales on this crocodile.

Many reptiles **hatch** from eggs. A turtle egg is tough and leathery.

Some reptiles, like this snake, lie in the sun to get warm.

Features of Reptiles

- have scales
- are cold-blooded
- have a backbone

Fish

Fish come in many colors, sizes, and shapes. A fish's shape helps it move easily through the water. So do its fins. Scales protect a fish's body. **Gills** are special body parts that fish use to breathe underwater. Like reptiles, fish are cold-blooded.

Sharks are a kind of fish. Sharks do not have scales.

scale

fin

gill

Most fish hatch from eggs.

Features of Fish

- live in water

- have gills

- usually have scales

- are cold-blooded

- have a backbone

Amphibians

Amphibians are another group of animals. Frogs, toads, and salamanders belong to this group. Unlike fish and reptiles, they do not have scales.

An amphibian begins life as an egg. Then it goes through two more stages in its life cycle: a **larva** stage and an adult stage. When an amphibian is in the larva stage, it has gills and lives in water. When it grows into an adult, it develops lungs and lives on land. This process of change is called **metamorphosis**.

A salamander is a kind of amphibian.

A tadpole is the larva stage of a frog.

Features of Amphibians

- live part of life in water
- go through metamorphosis
- have skin without scales
- are cold-blooded
- have a backbone

Birds

Most birds can fly. Some birds can swim, too. Some birds, like the ostrich, cannot fly or swim! They walk or run to get around.

All birds lay eggs. All birds also have feathers. Some feathers help birds fly, and some feathers help birds stay warm.

An eagle's feathers help it fly.

Birds are **warm-blooded**. This means that their bodies stay about the same temperature, no matter what the temperature is around them.

Birds hatch from eggs.

A penguin's feathers help it stay warm.

Features of Birds

- have feathers
- hatch from eggs
- are warm-blooded
- have a backbone

Mammals

Mammals are another group of animals. Most mammals have fur or hair, like dogs and cats. Some mammals, such as elephants, have just a little hair on their bodies.

Most mammals give birth to live babies. The babies drink milk from their mothers. Baby mammals need care from their parents. Some adult mammals teach their young how to find food.

Some mammals, like this whale, live in water.

Features of Mammals

- **often have fur or hair**
- **feed their babies milk**
- **are born live**
- **are warm-blooded**
- **have a backbone**

Animal Features

Look at this table of animal features.

Feature	Reptiles	Fish	Amphibians	Birds	Mammals
hatch from eggs	often	usually	usually	yes	rarely
have a backbone	yes	yes	yes	yes	yes
are warm-blooded	no	no	no	yes	yes
feed their babies milk	no	no	no	no	yes
have scales	yes	usually	no	no	no
have feathers	no	no	no	yes	no
have fur or hair	no	no	no	no	yes

Play an Animal Features Game

- Take turns with a partner.

- Partner 1 tells a fact about an animal group.

- Partner 2 tells the same fact about another animal group. Then Partner 2 tells a new fact about the animal group.

- Continue telling facts about each animal group.

Here's an Example

Partner 1: Birds hatch from *eggs*.

Partner 2: Amphibians hatch from *eggs*, too.

Amphibians have *gills* when they live in water.

Partner 1: Fish have *gills*, too.

Fish have *scales*.

Partner 2: Reptiles have *scales*, too.

Reptiles have *backbones*.

Partner 1: Mammals have *backbones*, too.

Glossary

cold-blooded   having a body temperature that changes with the temperature of the surroundings

gills   parts of a fish that let it take in oxygen from water

hatch   to break out of an egg

larva   an early stage in the life of an amphibian (for example, a tadpole is the larva stage of a frog)

metamorphosis   the change of form some animals go through

vertebrate   an animal that has a backbone

warm-blooded   having a body temperature that stays constantly warm